Getting and Staying Organized

MW00743533

Getting and Staying Organized

CORINNE R. LIVESAY

Business Skills Express Series

IRWIN
Professional Publishing

MIRROR PRESS

Burr Ridge, Illinois
New York, New York
Boston, Massachusetts

IRWIN
Concerned About Our Environment

In recognition of the fact that our company is a large end-user of fragile yet replenishable resources, we at IRWIN can assure you that every effort is made to meet or exceed Environmental Protection Agency (EPA) recommendations and requirements for a "greener" workplace.

To preserve these natural assets, a number of environmental policies, both companywide and department-specific, have been implemented. From the use of 50% recycled paper in our textbooks to the printing of promotional materials with recycled stock and soy inks to our office paper recycling program, we are committed to reducing waste and replacing environmentally unsafe products with safer alternatives.

This publication is designed to provide accurate and authoritative information in regard to the subject matter covered. It is sold with the understanding that neither the author or the publisher is engaged in rendering legal, accounting, or other professional service. If legal advice or other expert assistance is required, the services of a competent professional person should be sought.

From a Declaration of Principles jointly adopted by a Committee of the American Bar Association and a Committee of Publishers.

Mirror Press:	David R. Helmstadter
	Carla F. Tishler
Editor-in-chief:	Jeffrey A. Krames
Project editor:	Jean Lou Hess
Production manager:	Laurie Kersch
Designer:	Laurie Entringer
Art manager:	Kim Meriwether
Art studio:	Electra Graphics
Compositor:	Alexander Graphics, Inc.
Typeface:	12/14 Criterion Book
Printer:	Malloy Lithographing, Inc.

Library of Congress Cataloging-in-Publication Data

Livesay, Corinne R.
    Getting and staying organized / Corinne R. Livesay.
        p.   cm. — (Business skills express series)
    ISBN 0-7863-0254-2
    1. Time management.   I. Title.   II. Series.
    HD69.T54L59   1994
    650.1—dc20   94–6257

Printed in the United States of America
1 2 3 4 5 6 7 8 9 0 ML 1 0 9 8 7 6 5 4

PREFACE

The downsizing mania that has affected most of corporate America in recent years has dramatically changed most people's jobs. Perhaps your job description today reflects a combination of what formerly were two or three different jobs. Unfortunately, as the workforce declines, the workload does not. And you may be expected to be much more productive today than you were even a short time ago.

As you will learn from this book, organizing skills that are developed and used properly can dramatically improve your personal productivity to help you handle the increased demands of your job. In addition, organizing skills can improve your self-confidence as you learn to control your environment instead of letting your environment control you. Having the reputation as a well-organized person can also improve the professional image you project to clients and co-workers. This book also shows how being well organized can have a positive impact on career opportunities.

The six organizing guidelines you'll learn will help you develop and fine-tune your organizing skills. *Getting and Staying Organized* may be one of the most important things you can do for yourself and your career.

Corinne R. Livesay

ABOUT THE AUTHOR

Corinne R. Livesay is Assistant Professor of Management and Director of Business Internships at Liberty University in Virginia. As an educator and consultant, Ms. Livesay has led seminars in business writing and time management. She is an active member of the American Society for Training and Development and has been a trainer in management and communication courses for the American Management Association Extension Institute.

Ms. Livesay has published several training supplements and application exercises for a college textbook on supervision, as well as a student exercise book to accompany a management and organizational textbook.

ABOUT IRWIN PROFESSIONAL PUBLISHING

Irwin Professional Publishing is the nation's premier publisher of business books. As a Times Mirror company, we work closely with Times Mirror training organizations, including Zenger-Miller, Inc., Learning International, Inc., and Kaset International, to serve the training needs of business and industry.

About the Business Skills Express Series

This expanding series of authoritative, concise, and fast-paced books delivers high-quality training on key business topics at a remarkably affordable cost. The series will help managers, supervisors, and frontline personnel in organizations of all sizes and types hone their business skills while enhancing job performance and career satisfaction.

Business Skills Express books are ideal for employee seminars, independent self-study, on-the-job training, and classroom-based instruction. Express books are also convenient-to-use references at work.

CONTENTS

Self-Assessment

Are you as organized as you need to be at work? Completing this self-assessment will help you find out. Regardless of your final score, *Getting and Staying Organized* will help you use organizing skills to increase your efficiency and effectiveness on the job.

Rate yourself on each of the 10 items below using the following scale:

Questions	Almost Always	Some-times	Almost Never
1. The desk drawers I use most often are organized so when I go to that drawer to get something, I can put my hands on that item with little searching.	_____	_____	_____
2. At the beginning of an average day, I know what my most important tasks are for that day.	_____	_____	_____
3. By the end of an average day, I can say I have accomplished the most important tasks I set out to complete for that day.	_____	_____	_____
4. When I begin to work on one of my common tasks, I go to only one place to get all the materials, equipment, and so on that I need to complete the task.	_____	_____	_____
5. On an average day, I spend less than five minutes looking for things I use every day (keys, eyeglasses, pens, phone numbers, etc.).	_____	_____	_____
6. Within the past month I haven't missed any scheduled appointments or forgotten any significant dates.	_____	_____	_____
7. I typically have fewer than three newspaper or magazine issues lying around unread.	_____	_____	_____
8. No one within the past two weeks has had to remind me to do something I had promised to do but forgot.	_____	_____	_____
9. When I go through my mail on an average day, I open it, look at it, and make a decision on what needs to be done with it right then.	_____	_____	_____
10. Thinking that an item might come in handy someday does not keep me from throwing away items I no longer use.	_____	_____	_____

1 | What Can Organizing Skills Do for You?

This chapter will help you to:

- Understand what organizing skills are.
- Appreciate better how to achieve desired goals in your work.
- Learn how organizing skills can enhance your personal productivity and professional image on your job.

Kathleen Johnson was on the phone with an important client who asked why he hadn't received the information packet Kathleen had promised to send him more than two weeks earlier. Kathleen hastened to apologize for the delay and promised him she would get the packet out in this afternoon's mail.

As she hung up the phone, Kathleen looked at her cluttered, disorganized surroundings. She hadn't seen the top of her desk in months. Somewhere in those mounds of papers, file folders, unopened mail, and who knows what else, was the information she was looking for. She didn't have enough nerve to admit to Bill Eberhardt that she couldn't remember the specifics of what he wanted included in the information packet. Instead, she hoped she would be able to find that yellow legal-size pad of paper she had written the information on during their meeting.

As she began the scavenger hunt to track down the critical information, her boss showed up in the doorway. "Do you want to walk over to the meeting together?" Kathleen responded, "Listen, Pat, I've got to take care of getting some information

1

together for the Eberhardt deal. Why don't you save a seat for me, and I'll get there as soon as I can.'' Pat looked a bit put out. ''When Charlie calls one of his meetings, Kathleen, you know he makes a public spectacle of any department head who can't get his people to show up on time. We're going to have to come up with a way that we can get you up to speed with the rest of us—it seems like you're always running a half hour behind everybody else in the office.''

Kathleen mumbled her apologies and told Pat she would go to the meeting now and would take care of the Eberhardt matter after the meeting. She knew, however, that if Pat knew the full story, he would agree she should take care of it now. Kathleen decided, however, that she was already in enough trouble with Pat and hoped she would be able to get everything taken care of after the meeting . . . ■

WHAT IS ORGANIZATION?

Although Kathleen's situation focuses on the effects of disorganization, let's focus on organization. What comes to your mind when you think of the word *organization*. Use the space below to brainstorm:

_____

_____

_____

Some possibilities include the following:

- "A place for everything, and everything in its place."
- "The ability to coordinate resources to achieve goals."
- "A set of skills that help you to get your job done on time and within budget."
- "Having your act together."
- "The ability to process an assortment of information into a pattern that makes sense."

1

WHO IS ORGANIZED?

Do you think your co-workers have established reputations that reflect their level of organizing skills? Would you be able to rate each co-worker on the following scale? Where on this scale would your co-workers or your boss place you?

Totally Disorganized	Somewhat Disorganized	Organized	Very Organized	Totally Organized

What are some of the qualities or characteristics you have observed in the people you placed on the left half of the continuum (totally or somewhat disorganized)?

_____

_____

What have you observed in the people you placed on the right half of the continuum (very or totally organized)? By the way, it's appropriate to note here that although much of this book is directed to people who are disorganized, it is also for those who are overorganized. As you will learn in Chapter 2, being on the extreme right of this organizing continuum is to be *overorganized* and can be as much of a liability (albeit a different liability) as being totally disorganized.

_____

_____

Generally, the characteristics or qualities you listed that relate to an organized person would show a higher level of *efficiency* and *effectiveness* than those you listed for the disorganized person.

ORGANIZING SKILLS ON THE JOB

Organizing skills are essential to help meet three specific needs that exist in nearly every job. The first category of needs is your *own need*. For example, most tasks you perform each day require organizing skills to help you find what you need when you need it. If you have the "tools of your trade" in an organized, orderly arrangement, you can focus your energies on doing your job rather than on finding what is missing. In this way, you will be organized to meet your own needs. The second category of needs is *others' needs*. When co-workers or your boss, for example, can count on you to get them what they need quickly and efficiently, you are using your organizing skills to meet others' needs. Last, organizing skills help you fulfill *group needs*. When you're put in charge of a task that involves coordinating several people and many resources to accomplish a goal, you are using your organizing skills to help you and your group complete the task correctly and on time. You can see how your organizing skills come into play in meeting group needs.

Efficiency

Simply stated, *efficiency* is using your resources to their maximum capacity, thus reducing or eliminating waste. You've heard of fuel-efficient cars, energy-efficient heat pumps, and energy-saving appliances. In each of these cases, the design engineers worked to organize the parts that go into each product so that they would work together more efficiently and thus reduce the amount of energy needed to operate them. Consumers then should be able, for instance, to travel more miles on each gallon of gas in a fuel-efficient car than they would on a gallon in a model with a lower miles-per-gallon rating. Likewise, when you shop for a new refrigerator, you will see a yellow tag on each showroom model that will allow you to compare how much it will cost you per year to pay for the electricity for the various models you're considering. Appliance salespeople will tell you how those costs have come down over the years because the engineering designs are more efficient. Because of these more efficient designs, consumers realize maximum capacity from another resource: the money they're spending for energy. Every dollar spent for energy goes farther with an energy-efficient product than with one that is not.

Another way to say "increasing efficiency" is to say "reducing waste." When organizations set out to reduce waste, they are looking for ways to operate on fewer resources by getting more out of less. Outcomes of waste-reduction programs include the following:

- Changing the way departments are organized so that the work flow is smoother.
- Reorganizing the way work is done by eliminating unnecessary steps in the process.
- Reducing the number of employees while keeping the production levels the same.

In each of these examples, the work is reorganized so the resources going into the process are reduced and efficiency is increased.

Why Efficiency Is Valued in the Workplace

Employees obviously need to use organizational resources to their maximum capacity if they expect their company to turn a profit and stay in business. The resources available to employees to do their jobs—such as time, skills, money, supplies, and information—are more often better used by an organized person than by a disorganized one. People who arrange their resources haphazardly tend to either forget they have something or often cannot find it when they need it if they do remember having it. That's being disorganized and wasteful. On the other hand, organized people with organized resources will be more likely to remember what they have, be able to find it when they need it, and, therefore, use what they have to its maximum capacity.

People who use computers on their jobs are well aware of this principle. To use your computer files efficiently, they need to be kept up-to-date and categorized. If the computer files are not well organized, you will often forget that you have a file and waste time redoing work unnecessarily. Disorganized computer files can also lead to a great deal of wasted time trying to find a file that you know you have . . . somewhere.

Time, more than any other resource—perhaps because it is more likely to be limited—is one that everyone struggles to use efficiently. People who begin each day with schedules and prioritized to-do lists undoubtedly end their day with more tasks accomplished than a disorganized person who approaches each day with an "I-wonder-what-I-should-do-next?" approach. One can take control of the day to accomplish the most important tasks first; the other lacks focus and direction and will end up wasting a great deal of time.

Take a few moments to think of some work-related* examples of efficiency.

Describe a recent example in which you wasted a resource that you could have used if you were better organized.

_____

_____

_____

_____

_____

_____

Contrast your first example with an example of when you utilized a resource to its maximum capacity because of good organization.

_____

_____

_____

Effectiveness

Effectiveness is using organizing skills to help accomplish a task or reach a goal. Every task you set out to do or every goal you set out to achieve, whether you're working alone or on a team, requires that you organize the necessary resources. And an organized person is typically better able than

---

*Although this will not be noted at each exercise, feel free to relate the exercises in this book to your home environment rather than work. If you are already satisfied with your level of organization on your job but would benefit from better organization at home, this book is an excellent first step.

1

a disorganized person to coordinate a variety of resources—such as people, equipment, information, and materials—in a timely fashion to get the resources moving in the same direction toward completing a task or accomplishing a goal.

In this discussion, *goal* is used in a much broader sense than *task*. For every goal you set, you must accomplish a variety of tasks to move you toward that goal. For example, if you are a project manager for new product development, you and your team will have a broad goal that defines what kind of product you want to develop and the time frame in which you must accomplish it. As project manager, you would oversee the process of breaking the goal into smaller, more manageable tasks, assigning the necessary people and resources needed to complete each task, and coordinating all tasks with their assigned resources to keep on schedule and within budget. A good project manager uses organizing skills to coordinate a variety of resources to achieve a goal.

Have you ever been a member of a committee? Chances are good that you've had experiences on both extremes of what happens when a committee is formed to solve a problem. A negative experience ensues when the chairperson is disorganized; the group never seems to get off the ground. The disorganized chairperson calls meetings in which little is accomplished. A goal is never really clearly defined for the group. Although capable of solving the problem, the group never gets its resources coordinated, and the result is either an unsatisfactory solution or none at all. A positive experience takes place when the chairperson is organized, helps the group clearly define its goal, and is able to get everybody coordinated and moving toward achieving it. The group meetings have purpose, and you walk out of them feeling that your group is working well together and accomplishing what it's been assigned to do. In this second group, the outcome is typically more timely than the first group's, and the quality of the result is higher than the first group's result.

1

■ Think About It

Take some time to consider your own examples of effectiveness in your area of responsibility.

Describe a recent example in which inadequate organizing skills were a major reason that a goal was *not* successfully achieved.

_____

_____

_____

Contrast your first example with one in which you attained a goal, at least in part, because of good organizing skills.

_____

_____

_____

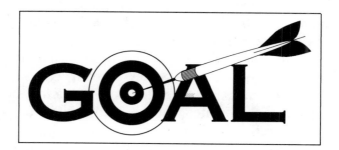

Confidence

Suppose you were to visit a doctor for the first time. As you walk into the waiting room, you observe a messy, unattractive area littered with tattered magazines. The receptionist takes several minutes to find your name in the appointment book because someone had written it in the wrong column. As you wait for the doctor in the examination room, you observe several open drawers filled with a variety of medical instruments tangled together. The counter is cluttered with tubes of ointment with no caps, some miscellaneous medical advice pamphlets, and some more medical instruments. The doctor comes into the room and sits down to talk with you and record some notes in your file before examining you. She can't find her pen, so she asks the nurse to get one.

As the patient in this scenario, how would you rate this medical practice (check one from each pair):

☐ **Efficient**   ☐ **Effective**
☐ **Inefficient**   ☐ **Ineffective**

Based on the information provided, how would you rate your confidence in this doctor as the best to treat your illness?

☐ **Low**   ☐ **Average**   ☐ **High**

First Impressions Count

Many people are strongly influenced by first impressions and find it difficult to place their confidence in a person who appears as disorganized as this doctor. Exceptions occur, of course, when someone is very competent in his or her profession despite appearing to be totally disorganized. It is likely, for instance, that you could place your confidence in a doctor such as the one described above if a trusted friend told you not to be put off by her disorganized appearance because she is an excellent doctor otherwise.

There is a correlation between the power of people's first impressions of your level of effectiveness and efficiency and how much confidence people will place in your abilities:

High effectiveness + High efficiency = High confidence
Low effectiveness + Low efficiency = Low confidence

Because it is more difficult to recognize competence in a disorganized person than in an organized one, it is important not to bury your true capabilities under an appearance of disorganization. Don't let others' first impression of you wrongly displace their confidence in your abilities. People argue that it is wrong to judge a book by its cover, but the fact is that many people will judge abilities based on first impressions. Make sure your first impression is that of an efficient and effective person.

Disorganized people usually project an incompetent and unprofessional image. They are often viewed as not having their "act together." Others often conclude, "How in the world can I place confidence in his ability to take on this new responsibility when he appears so incompetent at handling his current job?" For example, consider the most disorganized person in your group. Would your boss have enough confidence in that person to put him or her in charge of a critical project? The answer is almost certainly "no."

QUALITY OF LIFE

Being known as an efficient, effective, and confidence-inspiring employee is only one of the benefits derived from improving your organizing skills. Another benefit is increased self-confidence. Indeed, improving your organizing skills can improve your quality of life.

Here are some comments from those whose quality of life improved because of being organized:

- "Before I got organized, I would often get caught up in one small task for a long time and not have enough time to focus on the important areas of my job. Even my boss commented on how much more productive I've been lately."

- "When my surroundings are in order, I feel much more comfortable and in control."

- "It's amazing how much more work I'm getting done now that I've applied some organizing principles to my office and work area. I also feel like I'm projecting a much more positive professional image to my clients than previously."

These comments suggest the following connections among organizing skills, your self-confidence, and your job:

- *Experiencing improved personal productivity—being able to get more done in less time.* You will be able to get things done more quickly than you would if you are disorganized. You will be free to do the things you enjoy in all your new-found time.

- *Improving your self-confidence as you learn to control your environment instead of your environment controlling you.* When you work in an organized environment and can quickly find what you need when you need it, you will feel a greater sense of control than if everything around you is in chaos.

- *Projecting an improved professional image to clients and co-workers.* When people perceive that you are someone who has his or her act together, they will often place greater confidence in your abilities.

CAREER IMPLICATIONS

Few would argue against the notion that it can be beneficial to your career to be known as one who uses his or her resources to the maximum and can get jobs done on schedule within budget. Employees who can prove themselves in their current assignments are the ones sought out to take on bigger assignments. Improved organizing skills can play a key role in improving your job effectiveness and enhancing your reputation as a person who is in control and can get the job done. The remainder of this book will present six basic organizing guidelines that can help you improve your job performance.

- Guideline 1: Select What Should Be Organized
- Guideline 2: Unclutter Your Life
- Guideline 3: Break Organizing Tasks into Specific Steps

1

- Guideline 4: Establish a Simple System
- Guideline 5: Stay Organized
- Guideline 6: Be Only as Organized as You Need to Be

Following these guidelines on a daily basis will greatly improve your ability to get and *stay* organized.

Chapter Checkpoints

✓ Being well organized improves your efficiency, allowing you to reduce waste and maximize the use of your resources.

✓ Organizing skills improve your effectiveness on the job because you are able to coordinate resources to accomplish tasks and to achieve goals.

✓ People often will place greater confidence in your abilities if they observe an organized person rather than a disorganized one.

✓ You can experience quality-of-life improvements from being well organized by
  - Being able to get more done in less time.
  - Controlling your environment instead of letting your environment control you.
  - Improving the professional image you project to clients and co-workers.

✓ Being organized can lead to career advances.

2 | Select What Should Be Organized

This chapter will help you to: ─────────────

- Ignore the 80 percent of organizing activities that don't contribute to getting the job done.
- Focus on the 20 percent of resource organization that enables you to realize 80 percent of the value of getting organized.
- Identify the areas that you should organize that will result in the greatest benefits.
- Understand and use the 80–20 Rule.

Barbara Kingfisha determined that this would be the last time she would let her lack of organization be a source of embarrassment to her on her job. Barbara had about three different projects pending on her desk and surrounding surfaces when her boss, John Greeley, showed up unexpectedly with an important client. After introductions, John asked Barbara for a report she had written about two weeks earlier that contained some important information that he and the client needed to review quickly before a conference call scheduled in 10 minutes. Although Barbara did vaguely remember seeing it somewhere within the past day or two, she had no idea where the information was now. Her backup plan didn't serve her too well either: when she tried to find it on her hard drive, she couldn't remember what directory she had saved it under. She realized that she must have looked totally out of control as she first scrambled through stacks of papers on her desk and on the floor and then tried to find the report on her computer. John and the client finally had to leave without the information they came for.

Barbara knew she was overdue on organizing her office. She kept excusing her poor organization to lack of time and to too many pressing deadlines that were more important than getting organized. She knew, however, that if things didn't change drastically soon, she would be buried under the mess, never to be seen or heard from again! She was determined to get organized, but as she surveyed the monumental task before her, she just didn't quite know how to go about it. She didn't have a clue on where to begin . . . ■

FIRST THINGS FIRST

There's no way around it—getting and staying organized will require an investment of your time. There is no quick fix. However, investing your time in getting and staying organized is guaranteed to pay rich dividends. Therefore, you will find that the time you spend in developing and using your organizing skills will be returned many times over in the form of increased productivity, improved self-confidence, and enhanced professional image.

Before jumping in with both feet to start organizing your life, first identify the areas or resources that merit your investment of organizing time. You must carefully choose those areas that will give you the most benefit for the time you will spend in getting and keeping them organized. An understanding of the 80–20 Rule will help you make the best choices.

THE 80–20 RULE

An Italian engineer in the early 1900s named Vilfredo Pareto applied mathematical principles to social and economic phenomena, such as the concept that the majority of the world's economic wealth is owned by the minority of its people. His law of the "trivial many" and the "vital few" is referred to as the Pareto Principle or the 80–20 Rule. This rule states that 80 percent of the value comes from 20 percent of the resources—the "vital few"—while the remaining 20 percent of the value comes from 80 percent of the resources—the "trivial many." Here are some examples of the 80–20 Rule:

- 80 percent of the world's economic wealth is owned by 20 percent of the population.

- 80 percent of an organization's sales revenues comes from 20 percent of its product line. (This is the principle on which organizations such as Sam's Wholesale Club, Costco, Pace, BJ's Wholesale Club, and Price Club base their success. They work to carry only the 20 percent "vital few" products in their inventory; if a product doesn't turn over quickly enough, they stop carrying it.)

- 80 percent of sales comes from 20 percent of the total customer base.

- 80 percent of an organization's productivity comes from 20 percent of its workforce.

- 80 percent of your productivity comes from 20 percent of the things you do. At the end of a day, step back and examine actual results and all the different tasks you performed throughout that day. You would find that approximately 80 percent of the actual results were directly realized from approximately 20 percent of the tasks you performed. And the remaining 80 percent of the tasks you performed (opening mail, phone conversations, socializing, attending meetings, etc.) contributed the remaining 20 percent of the results.

This relationship may not always be exactly 80–20; it may be 70–30 or 85–15. The key principle is that in each situation there are a "vital few" activities that account for the largest share of the end result. The graph that follows illustrates the 80–20 Rule.

2

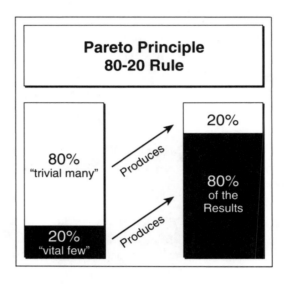

HOW DOES THE 80–20 RULE WORK?

Can you think of examples from your own experience that support this relationship described in the 80–20 Rule? For example, labor negotiators might notice the phenomenon that no matter how long the bargaining sessions have lasted, it seems that about 80 percent of the concessions made by both parties occur in the last 20 percent of negotiating time before the deadline. If you work with volunteers to coordinate an event, you will usually find that about 80 percent of the work is completed by about 20 percent of your volunteer base, those that are truly committed and willing to put in the necessary time and energy. Even something as mundane as the clothes you wear every day is related to the 80–20 Rule: many people realize that they wear their favorite clothes (20 percent of their wardrobe) about 80 percent of the time. They wear items from the remaining 80 percent the rest of the time. The 80–20 Rule usually applies to the shoes, ties, and earrings you wear as well. List some examples of how the 80–20 Rule applies to you.

_____

_____

_____

_____

_____

_____

2

The 80–20 Rule as applied to getting organized is illustrated in the following graph. The application, simply stated, is focus your energies on getting the high payoff areas organized, and don't worry about the rest. Using the 80–20 terminology, you can get 80 percent of the total value that organizing skills can bring to your life by having only 20 percent of the areas of your life organized, as long as the 20 percent qualifies as "vital few" or high payoff areas. Having the remaining 80 percent of your life organized contributes only an additional 20 percent benefit.

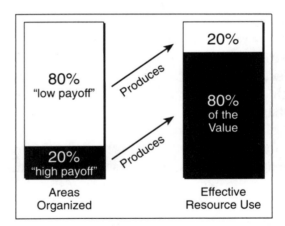

You can ask yourself two questions concerning this application of the 80–20 Rule:

- Have you identified the 20 percent, high payoff areas that will give you 80 percent of the value? This question is for those who have too much disorganization in their lives and perhaps believe that it is too

2

much work to get organized. They have based that belief on the wrong assumption that they must organize **everything** to get any benefit.

- Are you spending too much of your valuable time organizing the "trivial many" or low payoff areas? This question is for those who have too much organization in their lives. People in this group have not realized that the extra value they're getting is not normally going to justify spending the time and energy it takes to get and keep every nook and cranny of their lives organized. If they can rechannel the energy they're putting into low payoff activities to high payoff ones, then they'll get greater value for the time they're spending.

To help you apply the 80–20 Rule to your life, think of your immediate work area and make a list of everything in your area of responsibility that contains resources such as paper, supplies, information, materials, and so on. Include on this list every area or type of resource you use as part of your job. Some examples might include desktop, bookshelves, daily mail (regular and electronic), drawers, computer files (floppy disks, hard drives, CD-ROMs), client-tracking information, bins, closets, and other storage space. The more specific your list, the more it will help you in your organizing effort. For example, if you have five drawers in your desk, list them separately as "top right drawer," "middle right," "bottom right," "top left," and "bottom left." The reason for specificity will become apparent later on.

Some people reading this book might say, "I am a very well organized person when I'm at work; it's when I go home that all my organizing skills go out the window." You may wish to do this exercise using home instead of at work. Your list below might contain such areas as kitchen cabinets, bureau drawers, closets, garage, household recordkeeping, and so forth. If you would get the most benefit out of this book by achieving a more comfortable level of organization in your home, then you may choose to complete the exercises in this book applying them to your home setting.

Now it's time to make your list:

_____
_____
_____
_____
_____
_____
_____
_____
_____
_____
_____
_____
_____
_____
_____
_____
_____
_____
_____

SELECT HIGH PAYOFF AREAS

Review the list you just created and determine which areas are high payoff areas. Here are some examples and principles to guide you in your selection process:

- If your desk has five drawers, it's highly unlikely that every one of them has equally important items in it or that you use each drawer the same number of times each day. In reality, you probably rarely use two of those drawers because they contain items you refer to no more than once a week. You further realize that on average you use a third drawer no more than once a day. That leaves the final two drawers as the ones you access many times a day because they contain important items or important information that you need every day. You need to categorize the two drawers you use regularly as high payoff areas. The other three drawers are considered low payoff areas.

2

- You may use your desktop all the time, while the tops of your filing cabinets have things on them you use maybe once a week. Therefore, your desktop is a high payoff categorization, and the filing cabinet tops are not.

- Some people use the phone rarely on their job so having their telephone information carefully arranged, up-to-date, and easily accessible is not very important. This would *not* be a high payoff area for these people. On the other hand, those who sometimes feel the phone is a permanent extension on the side of their head would greatly benefit from having a very well-organized system for accessing accurate information quickly and easily. Telephone information would be a high payoff area for such people.

- Not every room or area in your home is a high payoff area. For example, the living room that you and your family use daily and where visitors spend most of their visit in is a high payoff area that demands more of your organizing time than a storage area, such as a basement or extra bedroom, which you use much less frequently.

The premise of these examples is that you will quickly recoup the time you spend getting a regularly used area organized. For example, suppose you have a desk drawer that is in total chaos right now. Every time you open that drawer, it's a major accomplishment to actually find what you're looking for; it takes you an average of two minutes to find what you need each time you go to that drawer. Because you use that drawer 8 or 10 times a day, you decide it would be a wise use of your time to take 15 minutes to get its contents organized. With the improved organization, you can find what you need within a few seconds each time you open the drawer. Based on these before and after "search times," you would recoup within two days the 15 minutes you spent getting it organized. From that point on, assuming you keep the drawer organized, you will start saving time that you would have spent in searching. Furthermore, you will have eliminated, or at least dramatically reduced, a source of irritation in your life.

Suppose, on the other hand, that you decided to spend the 15 minutes on a drawer you use only once a week. This drawer would be a low payoff area because it would take seven to eight weeks to make up for the 15 minutes of organizing time. Obviously, you will get much more value from your organizing time by focusing on those areas you use most often.

There is nothing wrong with organizing the drawer that you use only once a week. And maybe if someday in the distant future you're bored to death and have nothing else making demands on your time, you will decide to organize that drawer also. For now, however, it makes sense that it would be better to spend your time organizing those areas that will result in the highest payoff.

When selecting your high payoff areas, don't compare yourself with others. You should not choose an area, for example, just because someone you work with has a system you admire and want to emulate. Because everyone works differently, one person's high payoff area will not automatically be another person's. Make sure your choices are based on how you work. A high payoff area for you should be one that

- Is used many times a day.
- Contributes a substantial amount to your ability to perform your job.
- Is an integral part of your work flow.

APPLY THE 80–20 RULE TO YOUR JOB

Based on these examples and principles, review your list and check anything that you qualify as a high payoff area. Remember that your choices should be limited to about 20 percent of the items on your list. If you've checked more than 20 percent of them, you need to reexamine the items checked to make sure that each one represents a high payoff area for you and the way you work.

2

Because the checked items will keep you focused on where you will benefit most from getting organized, take the time now to rewrite the high payoff areas from the checklist on a separate list below:

_____

_____

_____

_____

_____

For the rest of the book, identify ways to get organized in these specific areas. Go for the 80 percent, high payoff value up front; there's no sense in wasting your energies on low payoff organizing projects.

Chapter Checkpoints

✓ Getting and staying organized will require an investment of your time.

✓ Organizing the right things, however, will quickly recoup the time spent getting organized.

✓ The 80–20 Rule helps identify what the right things are.

✓ The 80–20 Rule teaches that
- You can get 80 percent of the total value that organizing skills can bring to your life by having only 20 percent of the most important high payoff areas organized.
- Having the remaining 80 percent organized contributes only an additional 20 percent benefit.

3 | Unclutter Your Life

This chapter will help you to:

- Analyze your cluttered areas and determine the main cause for clutter.
- Understand the anticlutter principles.
- Reduce clutter by using the anticlutter principles.
- Adopt a clear, simple method to control mail clutter.

Brent Martinez had a few spare minutes before he had to go to the departmental meeting, so he decided to catch up on filing. Nearly every drawer he opened exceeded maximum capacity or was approaching it, and he had to virtually stuff some things into the drawers. "I've been on this job just a year and a half," he thought, "and I've already managed to fill up three file cabinets. I guess it's time to requisition another one." Brent had always taken great pride in his expertise at saving things, dating to when he was a child and had dresser drawers, closets, and crates full of schoolwork and other memorabilia he collected throughout the years. The only trouble was that often he couldn't prove he had saved something because he couldn't find it. Come to think of it, that seems to be the biggest problem with his filing system in his office, too. "Oh, well," he said to himself, "my filing system will improve once I get that fourth filing cabinet in here . . . I am going to have to work out a new floor plan, though, to figure out how to fit it in." ■

3

CLUTTER: A MAJOR ROADBLOCK

Before you begin organizing one of the high payoff areas you identified in Chapter 2, you must anticipate the major roadblock that may keep you from getting organized. In Brent's case, he has the habit of hanging on to everything. He no longer makes good decisions on what to save and what to keep; he just saves everything and solves the problem by requisitioning more filing cabinets. Just because something is in a filing cabinet, however, does not guarantee that it is organized. Brent, for instance, can rarely find what he is looking for. It is doubtful that his filing cabinets will ever be organized unless he learns to unclutter them.

Clutter, as used here, refers to hanging on to unnecessary things that can

- Lead to working in a state of chaos.
- Create an uncomfortable and depressing work area.
- Cause you to waste time searching for misplaced items.
- Hamper organizing efforts.

Here's an extreme case scenario: You walk into Daniel Herak's cluttered work area and observe no sense of orderliness in what you see. You ask yourself how he can stand working in all this mess. He must waste hours looking for things when he needs them. The only way he'll ever get any order in this office is if he were to dynamite the place and start from scratch.

A more "average person" scenario might be this: You decide it's finally time to get that high payoff drawer organized. When you try to open it, you have to borrow a co-worker's ruler to push down the drawer's contents because something is jammed and keeping it from opening all the way. When you finally get the drawer open, you find the clutter and mess to be so overwhelming that you talk yourself into tackling this project another day.

The fact is, most people get sidetracked from getting organized if there is too much clutter. Without a doubt, clutter is a major roadblock that gets in the way of getting organized.

GET RID OF CLUTTER

The best way to deal with clutter is to get rid of it. Getting rid of clutter before getting an area organized has many benefits:

- The clutter reduction will eliminate one excuse for not getting organized.
- You will save time in your organizing effort because you will have fewer items to organize.
- Setting up a good system will be easier because you won't have so many items to deal with. (You will cover setting up a good system in Chapter 5, Establish a Simple System.)
- Because clutter can destroy any good organizing system, you will find that maintaining your system will be easier if you don't allow clutter to accumulate. (Maintaining your system is covered in Chapter 6, Stay Organized.)

WHY DO PEOPLE HAVE A CLUTTER PROBLEM?

Most people would have no trouble listing five or six areas they would categorize as "cluttered." Some examples are filing cabinets, closets, desktop, and drawers. Start your list naming cluttered places at work; if you can't come up with six from work, you could probably finish your list with examples from home.

1. _____

2. _____

3. _____

4. _____

5. _____

6. _____

As you examine each of the areas you listed, ask yourself this question: "Why am I having a clutter problem with this particular area?" For example, if you have a section in your desk drawer that is overflowing with pens, what is causing the clutter problem? Or if your desktop is cluttered, look at the things on your desk to see if they have common characteristics that might help you determine the main source of the clutter or why you allowed this to happen. Complete the chart below for the cluttered areas you've identified:

Cluttered Area	Cause of Clutter

Although there are many ways to describe them, most causes of clutter are related to two patterns.

Hanging On to Unnecessary Things

Some people were born with "pack rat" tendencies, and it's very difficult for them to part with their belongings. They are known to get emotionally attached to their belongings and keep almost everything they have ever owned even after it has outlived its usefulness. They can't part with anything that reminds them of a special person or special moment. You can spot these people easily. They're the ones who save such things as the last five years' worth of their favorite magazine. Their kitchen cabinets are full of every imaginable color and style of glass. This hodgepodge of drinking glasses represent "the survivors" from the sets they've owned through the years. Among the remains are two from the set that was Aunt Bessie's wedding gift in 1978, four from the set Mom and Dad got them in 1985 for Christmas, and one survivor from the set of four souvenirs they bought for the kids when they visited Disney World in 1990. They still have every program and every laminated name tag they've ever gotten from every conference and seminar they've ever attended. They have a drawer, and it's usually quite large, in which they've collected spare parts to unknown things. They still keep every pair of shoes they've had since high school. They may say:

- "Hang on to everything because you never know when it might come in handy."
- "Never get rid of any sentimental mementos."
- "Only wasteful, pampered people who have had everything given to them in life get rid of things that still have value to them."

Putting Off Making Decisions

When you put off deciding what to do, you're actually making a decision; that decision is that you will make a temporary but significant decision. That is, the temporary decision has consequences. Some examples of a temporary decision follow:

- "I'll put this book here for now."
- "I'm in a hurry, so I'll just lay this here and take care of it later."
- "I don't feel like dealing with this right now. I'll just set it here until I'm more in the mood to handle it."
- "I better not throw this away now because I'll probably get to it one of these days."

This procrastination can lead to clutter. Obviously, there are times when everyone has to put off making a decision; however, procrastination should be the exception rather than the rule. You will find that people with lots of clutter in their lives procrastinate most of the time, and it's rare for them to make a decision immediately.

Besides creating clutter, temporary decisions are an admission that you will handle an item more than once, thus increasing your workload unnecessarily.

ANTICLUTTER PRINCIPLES

Methods for overcoming clutter are called anticlutter principles. The following rules can help you control the clutter in your life.

1. Set Limits

If you limit the number of things that contribute to your clutter, you can eliminate its source. For example, keep only the last two issues of your favorite magazine. Select your top seven pairs of shoes and give the rest to charity. Before you buy another pair, be willing to give up a pair you already own. Applying this principle to the opening vignette, Brent should set a limit on the number of filing cabinets he actually needs and not exceed that number. For example, let's assume he determines that two four-drawer filing cabinets are the maximum he needs. When space becomes a problem, he should reduce the clutter in the filing drawers by throwing out items he no longer needs to save. Better yet, he should make wiser decisions about what goes into the filing cabinets in the first place.

2. Analyze Usage

As a general rule, if you haven't used something within the past year, get rid of it. You set yourself up to have clutter if you keep things because they might come in handy someday. Everyone has experienced needing something only a short time after having gotten rid of it. Because of those mistakes, some people decide never to risk having that situation take place again, so they hang on to everything. Taking this approach, however, is taking risk aversion to an extreme. There is a balance between throwing things away haphazardly with little consideration of their value and never throwing anything away. Find the balance that's easiest for you to live with and that will help you reduce the clutter in your life. Besides, people who never throw out anything will have so much clutter that they will have actually defeated their purpose in keeping everything. That is, when the "come-in-handy" day finally arrives, they'll have so much clutter from saving everything that they'll rarely be able to find what they're looking for! That's what happened to Brent in the opening vignette.

3. Be Careful of Oversentimentalizing

Sometimes people keep things for what they say are "sentimental" reasons, when in reality it's really a matter of keeping something out of a sense of obligation or guilt. For example, keeping a wall hanging you detest that your aunt gave you for a wedding gift because you don't want her to notice it's missing next time she comes over is keeping something out of a sense of guilt. On the other hand, your grandmother may have given you a family heirloom necklace that's been in the family for generations. Although the necklace isn't exactly your style and you rarely wear it, you will always keep it—not out of a sense of obligation but rather because of its sentimental value. Remember, too, that if you save everything over the course of your life that reminds you of every positive event, special person you've known, or memorable place you've been, you're virtually guaranteed to have to live the rest of your life in a state of clutter.

4. Give Items with Value to Someone Who Could Still Use Them

When reducing clutter, you will often decide to get rid of items that still have some value. Take the time to get them where they can still be used. For example, community organizations will gladly accept clothing and other items to pass along to those who need them. You could give the books you're never going to read to the library or sell them to a bookstore that buys and sells used books. Hospitals, jails, and nursing homes are full of people who would enjoy being able to read your old magazines. And there is always the recycling option. Don't rush to throw away items that are still useful.

5. Handle Things Only Once

When you have something to put away, make a decision immediately about where it should go or who should get it. Because the item goes right where it needs to go and is not temporarily placed on a pile on the desk, on a chair, or on a table top, encouraging such a habit will reduce clutter. Besides reducing clutter, developing the habit of handling things only once will save you considerable time by reducing your workload. Anytime you handle something more than once you increase your work unnecessarily.

Solve These Clutter Problems

To help you apply some of these principles, practice solving the clutter problems described below.

Problem 1: Kara's Clutter Problem

Kara has a section in her desk drawer that is overflowing with pens. After rummaging through the pile and not being able to find her favorite one, she wastes the next several minutes looking everywhere for her favorite. Finally, she goes back to the drawer and selects from the 30 pens the one she settles for, choosing it because it looks newer than some of the others.

Cause: What's at the root of Kara's pen clutter? Because the pens still work, she feels that she had better hang on to them—even though she doesn't like writing with them and having 30 pens is only causing clutter in her drawer.

Solution: (What solution would you recommend for this clutter problem?)

_____

_____

_____

Problem 2: Katie's Clutter Problem

Katie gets frustrated every time she has to find something on her cluttered desk. Just this morning her boss asked her for some specific information from a report that she had received in the mail two or three days earlier. She remembered skimming the report the morning it arrived along with the other mail she received that day. Now if she could only remember what else came in the mail that day so she could make some associations and figure out which pile to start looking through first.

Cause: Why is Katie's desk such a mess? She has gotten into the habit of idly looking through her mail each day and laying it aside to deal with later. Because many things interfere with her getting back to dealing with it later, sometimes one or two weeks' worth of mail piles up before she gets backs to it.

Solution: (What solution would you recommend for this clutter problem?)

_____

_____

_____

(Suggested answers are shown on pages 37–38, after we examine a common clutter-causer, below.)

MAIL AND THE 4-D METHOD

At some point each of us has to take control of the mail in his or her life. The case of Katie's missing report is one example of how easy it is to let mail create clutter in your life and disrupt your work. Two factors contribute to mail clutter:

- Mail arrives most every day—and in the case of electronic mail (E-mail), more than once a day; therefore, it is one of the more consistent sources of clutter.
- Because there is so much of it—with little promise of that changing in the near future—mail can be one of the largest sources of clutter.

The best way to conquer the clutter that can be generated from your mail is to make a decision about what to do with each item the first time you look at it. Consider using the **4-D Method** for making quick decisions on each piece of mail. This method identifies four options:

1. *Don't open it.* Most "junk mail" doesn't even deserve the time it would take to open the envelope and skim its contents. Of course, you may miss valuable information by throwing out everything that has "bulk rate" postage on the envelope. One way you can recognize "Don't open it" mail is by identifying it as the second or third mailing you've received from the same company, and you already know it isn't something you need to open again. Other times the advertisement printed on the outside of the envelope may provide enough information to indicate that you need read no further.

2. *Discard it.* Some mail you will have to open before you will know whether to throw it out. It is far better to throw it away the first time you look at it than to let it sit on your desk for two months before you throw it away.

3. *Designate for action.* You will need to act on some mail. For example, some people find it helpful to have several hanging file folders in a drawer close to their desk where they can easily drop in the mail that will need to be processed further. Some appropriate file folder labels are

Correspondence to be Answered, Papers to be Filed (choose this option with care because filing everything that may come in handy someday definitely creates clutter), and Items to be Read Later. Because invoices you receive at work are generally referred to the accounting office, a Bills to be Paid folder isn't necessary. If you're setting up a system at home, however, you would want to include a bills folder. That way when you sit down to write checks once or twice a month, you can pull out your folder and have the bills in one place rather than having to dig through piles of mail on your desk to find the ones that came in since the last time you paid the bills. Based on the kinds of mail you get and the way you work, how should *your* folders be labeled?

_____

_____

_____

_____

_____

_____

4. *Direct it:* Some mail needs to be routed to another person. Sometimes the routing is for FYI (For Your Information) purposes only. Other times you may be directing it to another person for him or her to take the action. It is best to do this immediately and get it off your desk. (The invoice being routed to Accounts Payable is one example.)

Following the 4-D Method every time you handle your daily mail will help you take control of a major source of clutter and be more productive in the process.

Anticlutter in Action

Looking back at Kara and Katie's experiences on pages 34–35, let's consider some solutions.

Problem 1.   Using the anticlutter principles, Kara should begin by going through the pens and discarding any pens that no longer write. Next, she should *set limits* on the number of pens she will keep in her drawer to four

3

or five. Before she adds another to the pile, she should be willing to give up one she already has. *Analyze usage* by realizing that she doesn't even use most of the pens. Her limit of four or five should include her favorite pen and three or four others she has used recently that she also likes to write with. Finally, she should *give items with value to someone who could still use them* by taking the pens that still work well and returning them to the office supply closet for others to take next time they need another pen.

Problem 2.   The anticlutter principle that would help Katie most is to *handle things only once*. She should go through her mail daily and make a decision where it should go or what should be done with it the first time she looks at it. The 4-D Method options should guide her in her decision-making process: *Don't open it. Discard it. Designate for action. Direct it.*

Chapter Checkpoints

✓ Because clutter is a major deterrent to getting organized, you must get rid of it.

✓ Most clutter is caused from
  - Hanging on to unnecessary things.
  - Putting off making decisions.

✓ The Anticlutter Principles are:
  - Set limits.
  - Analyze usage.
  - Be careful of oversentimentalizing.
  - Give items with value to someone who could still use them.
  - Handle things only once.

✓ The 4-D Method helps you control the clutter that results from mail:
  - **D**on't open it.
  - **D**iscard it.
  - **D**esignate for action.
  - **D**irect it.

4 | Break Organizing Tasks into Specific Steps

This chapter will help you to: ────────

- Contrast productive and counterproductive procrastination.
- Understand how procrastination can keep you from getting organized.
- Explain the antiprocrastination principles.
- Use the antiprocrastination principles to break organizing tasks into specific steps.

"When will I ever learn my lesson?" Petros Girian asked himself for the umpteenth time. He reviewed what had transpired since last month's meeting as he walked down the long corridor toward the conference room. After waiting until the last possible moment to begin working on his presentation for last month's meeting and not doing a very good job in the process, he had vowed that he would get started earlier this month. He decided to set up a system for organizing the information so pulling it together each month would not be a major undertaking.

Yesterday, however, he found himself frantically searching databases and calling other members on the team to get the information he needed. He ended up pulling an "all-nighter," as he had so many other months, to try to get ready for this morning's presentation. As the Pluto project manager, one of his more visible roles was the monthly project update presentation to several top executives and board members, as well as to representatives from the company's major suppliers. Even though it was a critical function of his job, Petros just couldn't seem to overcome his procrastination in getting things organized each month. If only there was somebody on the Pluto Project Team to whom he could delegate the responsibility for this monthly presentation . . . ■

TYPES OF PROCRASTINATION

Because procrastination can stand between you and your goal of getting organized, you will need to overcome this barrier. You will be better able to overcome it if you thoroughly understand it.

Productive Procrastination

Productive procrastination occurs when you put off taking care of something that you have determined is a low priority or low payoff activity. For example, when you return from lunch and check your phone messages on voice mail, it is productive procrastination to return the most important calls first and procrastinate, or delay, returning those of lesser priority.

Counterproductive Procrastination

Counterproductive procrastination occurs when you put off taking care of something that you know is a high priority or high payoff activity. For example, if you delay returning a high payoff phone call to an important client, that behavior is counterproductive procrastination. Likewise, when Petros put off setting up a system for organizing the information he needed for the monthly presentation, he was practicing counterproductive procrastination.

An Important Difference

Procrastinating at getting a high payoff area organized is counterproductive procrastination. If you did organize, you would quickly recoup the time it took you to get organized and would start "earning" extra time.

4

Therefore, putting it off is counterproductive. On the other hand, procrastinating on a low payoff area is productive procrastination because doing it would not give you very much value. Spending time organizing the top shelf in a closet you rarely use would be counterproductive, especially if there are other areas you use more regularly that are disorganized. Spend time on higher-priority areas and thus realize greater productivity from your time.

Identify three examples of **productive procrastination** that you have recently used on your job:

_____

_____

_____

Identify three examples of **counterproductive procrastination:**

_____

_____

_____

WHY DO YOU PROCRASTINATE?

As you look at your counterproductive procrastination list, reflect on your decision to not do something you knew really needed to be done. Do you see any pattern evolving?* How did you rationalize that you were making the best choice when you decided to procrastinate? What excuses did you make to justify your behavior? To rationalize wrong behaviors is to use "rational lies" to support those behaviors. All the excuses and rationalizations people use for putting off high payoff activities stem from two beliefs:

- You decided that it was an **unpleasant** task and that you would be happier if you avoided it.

---

*From this point on when the word *procrastinate* is used, it is referring to *counterproductive procrastination*. This negative meaning is, of course, its accepted meaning in general usage.

- You perceived that whatever you were avoiding was **too difficult**; thus, it would be easier to avoid it.

For example, if you're having trouble getting started on organizing a high payoff area, then you probably see the task as something you will not enjoy or as something too difficult. In extreme cases, you may think the organizing task is unpleasant **and** too difficult. But because procrastination can keep you from getting organized, overcoming it is a necessary ingredient in the getting-and-staying-organized process.

OVERCOMING PROCRASTINATION

There are no magic formulas for overcoming procrastination. You can develop some habits and attitudes, however, that will help you take control of procrastination instead of the other way around.

When the Task Is Too Unpleasant

Think about those tasks you're procrastinating on because they're unpleasant. For example, schoolteachers may procrastinate on grading papers because they find the task unpleasant. Next, see if answering a few questions about the area of procrastination you've identified convinces you that procrastinating may not be your best choice.

Your Area of Procrastination _____

No.	Question	Always	Sometimes	Never
1	Will the task get any easier by avoiding it?			
2	Will the task go away by avoiding it?			
3	Do you ever feel guilty while you're doing other things instead of what you know you **should** be doing?			

No.	Question	Always	Sometimes	Never
4	Do you fully enjoy your goofing off or leisure activity when you know you're doing that as a way of procrastinating on an important task?			
5	Have you ever put off doing something until the end of the day only to have that thing "nag" at you the entire day? And then when you finally took care of it at the end of the day and found out it wasn't anywhere near as awful as you had imagined, you wished you had started the day taking care of it so it wouldn't have put a cloud over your entire day?			

There are, of course, arguments in favor of procrastinating. For example, with questions 1 and 2, you could procrastinate so long that you no longer need to do the task or it doesn't have to be done as extensively as the original plan called for. Admittedly, however, that is a rare outcome of procrastinating. With questions 3 and 4, you may have a very high threshold for guilt and would not see these as good arguments in support of not procrastinating.

For many people, however, these are valid arguments for believing that when we choose to procrastinate, we are not making the best choice. Here, then, is the best approach you can take to overcome procrastinating because something is unpleasant.

THE BASIC PRINCIPLES

Antiprocrastination Principle 1: Just Do It!

This slogan, borrowed from a Nike commercial, succinctly captures the attitude necessary to overcome procrastination. Some may argue that this approach is too simplistic. Critics of the national antidrug campaign a few years ago said the same thing about the slogan "Just Say No." Society

4

sometimes overlooks the value of building character qualities of self-discipline and internal fortitude. These can serve as a source of strength to make the right choices. The next time you're confronted with the options of procrastinating or just doing it, remember this:

- Your avoidance of an important task will not make it any easier to do when the time comes that you can avoid it no longer.
- Avoiding the task will not make it go away.
- Avoiding the task will often cause you to feel guilty while you're doing something else.
- You will not fully enjoy a leisure activity that you choose to participate in while avoiding an important task.
- Most of the time, you will be better off doing the dreaded task first because your conscience won't nag at you while you're avoiding it, which often amounts to wasting time. For many people, putting off the dreaded task is a waste of time and energy, and their productivity will increase if they get it over with so they can move on to other priorities.

The real benefit of getting a task out of the way is that it frees you to do something you enjoy more. And you can do it without guilt and with a clear conscience that you've done what you're supposed to do.

Antiprocrastination Principle 2: Break One Major Task into Several Minor Ones

When the task is too difficult, one of the best habits you can develop is to break one major task into several minor tasks that are more easily achieved. When you think about doing the task, don't think of the whole task; just think about doing one small portion of it. There are several advantages to this approach:

- You will be more motivated to start a smaller project because the task has changed from something unmanageable and tough to something you should be able to handle without a lot of trouble.

- You may be putting off getting started because of fear of failure: the task is too difficult; therefore, you believe you won't be able to do it correctly. If the task is broken into smaller parts, logic follows that the fear of failure will diminish as well. One example of this is the advice given to someone who has to write a big report or thesis: *Don't get it right; just write it.* This slogan addresses why some writers have trouble getting started. They feel they have to get it perfect the first time they write it. Since that's an impossible assignment, they put off getting started. A better approach is to get something written as the first step. In subsequent steps, the writer can revise for improvement. Computer technology with its excellent simple revising capabilities alleviates the "too difficult" response to writing tasks.

- Half the battle is simply getting started. Sometimes you will find that once you get into a project, you will actually do much more than the minor task you set out to do. The success you've achieved in completing one small portion of it can provide the momentum you need to continue. Once you get into it, "you're on a roll" and want to keep going. Try this technique the next time you're putting off something: Set a timer for 10 minutes and tell yourself you will tackle this project for 10 minutes, after which time you will have an option to quit then or to continue. You may be pleasantly surprised to find that you will often opt to continue.

- Half of the fun of accomplishing a goal is rewarding yourself once it's completed. By breaking tasks down you'll have several points to reward yourself and celebrate your accomplishinents. You and a colleague can agree to go to your favorite place for lunch when you've reached one of the intermediate goals. Or maybe you can reward yourself with a round of golf or with the purchase of a CD you want. When you don't break down the tasks, you get only one reward! In addition, if you procrastinate until you reach a crisis mode of operation, you'll probably be too stressed out and worn out by the time the task is finished to enjoy a reward!

Is Speed the Answer?

Most "monumental accomplishments" are not executed and completed at lightning speed. Stop and think about your major accomplishments in the past six months: Didn't they come from having the discipline to be consistent and committed to doing a little bit every day to move you toward your goal? That's exactly how you need to approach the difficult tasks you're procrastinating on.

Stop thinking in terms of the entire task because you're just setting yourself up for being overwhelmed and discouraged, two conditions that almost always lead to procrastination. The old saying, "Life by the yard is hard; life by the inch is a cinch," certainly applies to overcoming procrastinating on important tasks.

If answering your mail is your "dreaded task" and you put it off until you reach a point where you can avoid the task no longer, you'll end up conducting a marathon session to get caught up. No wonder you dread it so much. Instead, discipline yourself to schedule two or three shorter sessions each week when you have fewer items to deal with each time. The task will become much more manageable, and you will be able to stay on top of it instead of being buried by it. The added benefit, of course, is that you'll be better able to satisfy your colleagues and clients with effective and prompt attention.

APPLICATION TO GETTING ORGANIZED

If procrastination is keeping you from getting high payoff areas organized, then you can benefit from applying the antiprocrastination principles:

- Just do it.
- Break one major task into several minor tasks that are more easily achieved.

The logic of the just-do-it approach tells you that since you've identified an area that you'd get great value from being organized, then the only way you're going to realize that benefit is to just do it! Go back to the high pay-off list you wrote on page 24 and copy that list here to remind yourself what you determined would be a "high payoff" organizing project:

_____

_____

_____

_____

_____

_____

4

Next put a check mark next to the one task that you think is the most important of the ones listed. Write the words *just do it* next to it. You will develop a plan to organize the task into specific steps in the next section of this chapter.

DEVELOP YOUR PLAN

Using the just-do-it high payoff area you selected above, follow these steps in breaking that organizing task into specific steps.

1. Schedule 15 to 20 minute time slots on your calendar once every couple of days that you call organizing time for this particular high payoff area. (You should never try to do an organizing task all at one time unless it is a small one.) Breaking the project into several specific steps will help you to avoid becoming overwhelmed with the entire task. You will move toward your organizing goal at a steady, realistic pace that even the busiest people should be able to fit into their schedule. This organizing program does not call for commitments of entire days of your time but just 15 to 20 minutes once every few days.

2. Unclutter the area following the anticlutter principles from Chapter 3, Unclutter Your Life:

- Set limits.
- Analyze usage.
- Be careful not to oversentimentalize.

4

- Give items with value to someone who can use them.
- Handle things only once.

3. Take whatever it is you're going to organize, and break the task down into however many steps it will take to complete it.

For instance, assume that you have targeted a bookcase with four shelves of books, notebooks, magazines, and journals that need to be organized.

You anticipate that it will take you about six 20-minute sessions (two hours) to complete the task. You normally start work at 8 every morning, and you decide that you will arrive early every Monday, Wednesday, and Friday for the next two weeks so that your 20-minute organizing time is completed by 8 AM.

Session 1 (Monday): Unclutter top two shelves by sorting through what you need to save and what you need to get rid of by following the anticlutter principles.

Session 2 (Wednesday): Unclutter the bottom two shelves.

Session 3 (Friday): Group all the notebooks on the bottom shelf according to subject area.

Session 4 (Monday): Because you have previously gotten rid of most of your magazines and journals after tearing out and filing those articles that you needed to keep for future reference, it doesn't take you too long to get your magazines and trade journals organized on the third shelf. You've only kept the latest three or four issues for each title, and it's pretty simple to arrange them in chronological order by title. You calculate it should take no more than 10 minutes for this task, so you sleep in a few extra minutes that morning (it's always good to be able to do that on a Monday).

Session 5 (Wednesday): Begin the sorting process by categorizing the books in your professional library under three broad subject areas.

Session 6 (Friday): In your last 20-minute session, you complete the sorting process and finish arranging the books. The top shelf contains all the books related to one subject area, and the second shelf is fairly equally distributed between the two remaining subject areas. You now have an organized bookcase that allows you to know what you have and to be able to put your hands on it quickly.

There is no problem if you find you have under- or overestimated the time the task would take. Obviously, if in this example, you finished the task early, you could simply cancel the remaining sessions. On the other hand, if you couldn't finish it in six sessions, you should be able, without too much inconvenience, to continue the scheduling pattern for however many extra sessions it takes.

4

■ Work Out Your Own Plan—Part 1

Now it's time for you to write out your own plan. Fill in the form below:

Area to be organized: _____

Estimated time to complete: _____

How many 15 to 20 minute sessions will you need to schedule? _____

When specifically will you fit these sessions into your schedule?

_____

For however many sessions you will need, identify what you want to accomplish in each session, unclutter, and then get it organized. If you're not sure what system to use in getting it organized, wait until after you've covered Chapter 5, Establish a Simple System, before providing any specifics about **how** you will get it organized. (This Work Out Your Own Plan exercise will be concluded at the end of Chapter 5.)

_____

_____

_____

_____

Chapter Checkpoints

✓ Putting off something that has a low priority is procrastinating in a productive way.

✓ Procrastination becomes counterproductive when you delay doing a high priority task.

✓ The two main reasons people procrastinate doing high priority tasks are because they believe that
- The task is too unpleasant.
- The task is too difficult.

✓ For tasks you perceive as unpleasant, use Antiprocrastination Principle 1: Just Do It!

✓ For tasks you perceive as too difficult, use Antiprocrastination Principle 2: Break one major task into several minor tasks that are more easily achieved.

5 | Establish a Simple System

This chapter will help you to:

- Distinguish between tidying up and getting organized.
- Understand that getting organized can be achieved with a simple system.
- Identify and adopt the system best suited to your organizing project.

Anthony Vista had nothing pressing on his schedule one morning and decided to use the time to get his office closet organized. His closet was where he put things he didn't know where to put because it was convenient to have a door to close to hide the mess. Lately, however, it had become tougher to get the closet door closed because of the clutter. Also, it sometimes took him as long as 10 minutes to find a critical item. He decided it was time to get control of the situation.

On downing his second cup of coffee at 8:25 AM, he tackled the job with great enthusiasm, picturing the closet with more order than mess. By 10:15 he congratulated himself on the progress he had made: the closet was completely empty now with the contents spread out in various random piles around the office. He also felt good that his trash can was overflowing with things he decided he no longer needed to keep. All the shelves and storage bins were dusted and cleaned up by 10:25, and he was now ready to start putting things back in the closet.

5

After two hours Anthony's enthusiasm waned. Maybe another cup of coffee would give him the boost he needed. On finishing another cup of coffee and handling a co-worker's question and two short phone calls, he had 50 minutes left to complete the task before lunch and his afternoon commitments. Anthony looked at the various piles scattered around his office and felt a strong urge to take an early lunch. He resisted the temptation, however, and instead aimed toward getting this project done in 45 minutes. He hurriedly went around his office, picked up the stacks of various items and placed them where he thought they would be best placed in the closet. Toward the end, however, his placement criterion stemmed from the answer to the question: "Where can I get this stack to fit?"

Forty-five minutes later, as he shut the door on his completed project, Anthony felt pretty good about his accomplishments:

- He had gotten rid of a lot of junk.

- It surely looked a whole lot better in there.

- The door closed with no trouble at all. ■

How Did Anthony Do?

Take a few minutes to analyze Anthony's organizing effort by answering a few questions based on what you've covered so far in the book:

Number	Question	Yes	?	No
1	Did Anthony select a high payoff area to organize?			
2	Did Anthony follow all the anticlutter principles?			
3	Did he follow Antiprocrastination Principle 1: Just do it?			
4	Did he follow Antiprocrastination Principle 2: Break one major task into several minor tasks that are more easily achieved?			

Suggested Answers

1. Yes. He made several trips to the closet each day and sometimes spent as much as 10 minutes searching for what he needed. It shouldn't take too long to recoup the time spent organizing, and then he'll start saving time thereafter.

2. ? The fact that he threw away some items he no longer needed may or may not indicate that he followed the anticlutter principles. For example, did he *set limits* when deciding he no longer needed something? Did he *analyze usage* for each item to determine whether he still needed it? Did he keep some of the clutter unnecessarily because of *oversentimentalizing*? There is no mention of *giving items with value to someone who could still use them.*

3. Yes. He took the opportunity of a free morning to tackle an organizing project he was avoiding.

4. No. Anthony should not have tackled such a major project in a marathon three- to four-hour session. Instead he should have scheduled many 15 to 20 minute time slots where he could organize, for example, one shelf at a time. The temptation is usually present to tackle the entire project at once. You may think: (a) I'll be able to see everything I have at once so it will be easier to get things grouped together when I put them away; (b) I better get this whole thing done while I've got the time and I'm in the mood. After all, how do I know when those two things will happen again at the same time? You will find, however, as Anthony did, that attempting to do everything at once, no matter how logical it may sound at the time, will usually produce disappointing results.

GETTING ORGANIZED OR TIDYING UP?

Now let's analyze Anthony's efforts while thinking about establishing a simple system. Choose the answer that best describes Anthony's accomplishment.

Number	Question
1	If people need to find something in Anthony's closet, are they likely to be able to do so easily?
	a. Yes. Now that everything is in such neat stacks, they should be able to locate what is needed.
	b. No. Because there is no particular pattern or system determining where things are located, it is highly unlikely other people will be able to find anything.
	c. ? It depends on whether Anthony is available to help search. It also depends on whether Anthony remembers the location of that particular item. And, of course, there is always luck. People might accidentally happen on the sought-after item right away.
2	When Anthony goes to the closet next, how will he find items?
	a. His memory ("Let me see if I can remember where I put that").
	b. His system ("Because I'm looking for the Anderson Project binder, it should be on the third shelf because that's where I put all the project binders").
3	How long will Anthony continue to be able to close the closet door easily?
	a. Probably not for long.
	b. It sounds as if he now has things under control, so getting the door to close should not be a problem in the future.

Suggested Answers

1. The best answer is "b." There is, however, a case for "c." as well.

2. a.

3. a.   A semblance of order will prevail for as long as his stacks stay neat. This means that after his memory fails him, Anthony will probably have trouble closing the door because he will have to start new stacks. Rummaging through the stacks to find what he's looking for almost guarantees that it won't take long before the closet looks the same as it did before Anthony "organized" it.

THE BEST INTENTIONS

Be careful what you identify as "getting organized." Even with the best intentions, Anthony did *not* get organized. That, of course, was his goal at the beginning. However, as the morning of the cleanup progressed, the organizing goal deteriorated to "tidying up." In part, he ended up tidying up because he tried to tackle too large a project all at once. Following the steps presented in Chapter 4, Break Organizing Tasks into Specific Steps, he would have had a better end result by doing a little at a time rather than by tackling an organizing project all at once.

In addition, perhaps Anthony was unaware of what options he had to get organized. Therefore, he could not select the best option to help him set up an organized system in his closet.

UNDERSTANDING ORGANIZATION CRITERIA   **5**

The chapter recommends that you *establish a simple system.* For an area to qualify as being organized rather than merely tidy, (1) it must be simple, and (2) it must follow a system. The following exercise will help you understand these two criteria more thoroughly.

Name an area you consider to be organized:

_____

Now ask yourself if that area meets the following criteria:

☐ **Yes** ☐ **No** *Is it simple?* Your organized area must be simple enough to meet two requirements: (1) others will understand it and (2) you won't have to spend a lot of time maintaining it. In the case of Anthony's organizing effort, it's easy to conclude that there is no simple way to guide people to certain desired items. People would need to consult Anthony, taking their time, as well as Anthony's. If anyone had to put things in the closet, he or she wouldn't know where. Once again, Anthony would have to get

5

involved. "Hey, Anthony, where do you want me to put this?" Of course, Anthony's response would probably be, "Wherever you can find room."

☐ **Yes** ☐ **No** *Does it qualify as a system?* Are the items arranged so that they follow a logical flow according to how they are used? This includes:

☐ **Yes** ☐ **No** *Are items placed in the location closest to where they will be used?* If you find yourself having to get up frequently to go to another area to get something you use for your job, then the system you have set up is not supporting how you do your work. Instead you should relocate the item in an area with easier access.

☐ **Yes** ☐ **No** *Do you keep the most-used items in the easiest-to-get-at locations?* The items Anthony uses most often should go on the shelves that are easiest for him to reach. If he were to place something he uses frequently on the top shelf so that he has to use a step ladder to reach it every time, that would obviously be inappropriate. Chances are, however, that if you examine where you have placed your most-used items, there may be some that are not in your easiest-to-get-at locations. Likewise, you probably have many infrequently used items taking up space in your easiest-to-get-at locations.

☐ **Yes** ☐ **No** *Do you group materials or equipment needed to complete common tasks all in one place?* To illustrate this principle, consider this fairly common task that many people perform around the holidays and for special occasions: wrapping gifts. Do you have trouble finding the right size gift box? Has someone in your family heard you say, "Who used the scissors last? I need them to cut this wrapping paper." Have you been known to use some of your child's Elmer's glue because you've searched high and low and haven't been able to find the tape? Are you positive that you bought some gold ribbon last time you wrapped a gift, but now you can't find it because you didn't store it with the wrapping paper? Does a task that should have taken you 2 minutes to do take you 20 because you didn't have all of the necessary items together in one place?

5

☐ **Yes** ☐ **No** *Have you taken advantage of the organizing aids available at your local store?* If the items in your top desk drawer are all mixed up, buy a desk tray with separate sections for paper clips, rubber bands, pens, and so on. If your floppy disks are scattered, buy a disk storage box with dividers for arranging your floppies according to one of the options outlined in the next question.

☐ **Yes** ☐ **No** *When appropriate, do you use alphabetizing, color coding, or numbering systems to set up a simple system?* In the case of organizing your computer disks, you could combine an alphabetizing and color coding system. First, group the disks by type and use the same color-coded label on all the disks belonging to each group. Second, within each color group, alphabetize according to the label title.

☐ **Yes** ☐ **No** *Do you learn about simple systems that work for your colleagues?* Because you and the people you work with often have similar resources to keep organized, it makes sense that you should share organizing techniques among yourselves.

SIMPLE SYSTEMS FOR YOUR DESK

One common work area that many people have to keep organized is a desk. This is probably one of the hardest areas for most people to keep organized. (There is even a National Clean Off Your Desk Day on January 11. Of course, cleaning it off is not the same as getting it organized.) Here are some ideas for setting up simple systems that can help you maintain orderliness (at least most of the time). These pointers are based on the questions outlined in the preceding section:

- *Is it simple?* An organized desk will not demand a great deal of your time to maintain. Therefore, you will want to set up uncomplicated systems that are based on your work flow and that do not require a great deal of effort on your part to use. If, for example, you use several different calendar systems to keep track of your appointments and other commitments, your system is too complicated. Choose one calendar system you like best that is simple to maintain, and keep all your activities recorded in it. It will save you duplication of effort in transferring information from several different sources, and it will decrease the likelihood that you will forget anything.

- *Are items placed in the location closest to where they will be used?* You should have a file drawer in your desk in which you keep your most commonly used file folders (color-coded hanging filing systems can be an efficient system). From time to time, it will be necessary to take out a folder you're no longer using frequently and place it in the filing cabinet you maintain for less-often-used items. Likewise, you will also need to add file folders as you take on new work assignments. Establish a rule: "Unless I'm currently working on the material in a particular file, I will keep all file folders in the drawer." Otherwise, it's too easy to have a mess of file folders all over the place, so that you can't ever seem to find the one you're looking for.

- *Do you keep the most-used items in the easiest-to-get-at locations?* Learn to use your drawers to store as much clutter as possible even for the things you use most often. Try to keep as much clear space on top of your desk as possible so you can spread out your work and so you won't be constantly knocking items on to the floor because of the clutter on top of your desk. For example, keep pens, staplers, and tape dispensers in an easily accessed drawer. Of course, there are exceptions. If you're working on something where you're using your stapler repeatedly, then you'd keep it on top of your desk until you've completed the task.

- *Do you group materials or equipment needed to complete common tasks all in one place?* Telephone messages and reminders scattered on your desk or written on scraps of paper are easily lost and create a cluttered look. Instead use a "to do" list where you jot down in one place the people to be called or the tasks to be completed and check off items as they are completed. In applying the principles discussed under the 4-D Mail Method that allows you to take control of your in-box, be sure you have the items close by for processing the mail quickly. For example, the trash can, the letter opener, routing slips, and the file folders for items to process further should all be readily available when you handle your mail each day.

- *Have you taken advantage of the organizing aids available at your local store?* Go to your local office supply store and select a system that will accommodate one place for all your telephone information. Instead of having business cards strewn about, having some phone numbers in your day timer, others on scraps of paper, and still others stuffed in your wallet, find a system that will allow you to keep all information together and near your telephone. Many people find the rotary card files to be the best way to systematize their business cards and other telephone and address information. In addition, if your phone has the capability to store frequently called numbers, take the time to program them. After using them several times, you will recoup the time spent programming them into your telephone. You will appreciate the time you will save in not having to look up the numbers and not having to dial them.

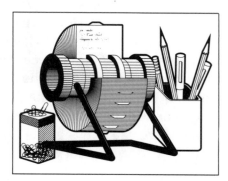

5

- *Where appropriate, do you use alphabetizing, color coding, or numbering systems to set up a simple system?* If you have a computer on your desk, then you can use alphabetizing and numbering systems to keep track of computer files on your hard drive. Say, for example, you have a DOS-based system and you're beginning a new project with a new client that you anticipate will take up much of your time for the next six months. Begin by creating a new directory under which you will store all the files you create related to this project. If the new client company is Echo Retail Group, you may choose to store the new directory on your D drive and call it ERG. For example, if the three categories of your work with clients are proposals, reports, and correspondence, create three sub-directories under ERG as follows:

- D:\ERG\PROPS (for proposals).
- D:\ERG\REPS (for reports).
- D:\ERG\CORR (for correspondence).

You could use numbering to save and retrieve your correspondence. Suppose the three people you write letters to are Becky Atwater, Grady McGee, and Bob Chiles. You could save the letters under the D:\ERG\CORR directory with their initials and the date of the correspondence. Therefore, your list of files under the D:\ERG\CORR directory might look like this:

File Name	Description
BA0712	Letter to Becky Atwater on July 12
BA0801	Letter to Becky Atwater on August 1
BC0627	Letter to Bob Chiles on June 27
BC0922	September 22 letter to Bob Chiles
GM0702	Letter to Grady McGee on July 2

- *Have you and your fellow workers shared information among yourselves about the simple systems that each of you is using?* Observing how others whose organizing expertise you admire are able to keep order on their desks may provide you with some excellent ideas to adopt.

Work Out Your Own Plan—Part 2

Review Work Out Your Own Plan—Part 1 that you developed on page 51. Finish that exercise by identifying what system or systems you will use to help you get that area organized.

What can you do to ensure that your system is simple to maintain? (This is particularly critical if others will need to use what you have organized.) _____

_____

_____

Determine the placement of items so they will be closest to where they will be used. _____

_____

_____

*List your most-used items and identify the easiest-to-get-at location
where each of those items should be placed.* _____
_____
_____

*Determine the items you need to group together because they will be
used together to perform a task.* _____
_____
_____

*If appropriate, identify what organizing aids you should purchase to set
up the most effective system possible.* If you aren't aware of any, perhaps a visit to your local office supply store will acquaint you with a
product that would be the perfect organizing aid. _____
_____
_____

Are any of these systems appropriate to get organized?

☐   alphabetizing
☐   color coding
☐   numbering

*To get ideas to help you set up simple systems, identify co-workers who
you think are well organized.* _____
*Determine whether you will observe their systems or ask them specific
questions about what has worked for them in areas where you need
advice or ideas to help you set up a simple system.* _____
_____
_____

Chapter Checkpoints

✓ Be careful that your organizing efforts amount to more than just exercises in tidying up.

✓ If you have established a simple system, it will meet these criteria:
- It will be easy for others to understand and use.
- It will be easy for you to maintain.
- You have placed items in locations closest to where they will be used.
- The most-used items will be in the easiest-to-get-at locations.
- Materials and equipment used to complete common tasks will be grouped together.
- You will use appropriate organizing aids.
- You will use alphabetizing, color coding, and numbering systems as appropriate.
- You will learn from your co-workers about the systems that have worked for them.

✓ Because the desk is such an important area for many workers, be sure that you have established simple systems in that work area that meet the above criteria.

6 Stay Organized

This chapter will help you to:

- Maintain your system once you get it established.
- Identify and characterize the maintenance habits you need to stay organized.
- Develop habits that will help you stay organized.
- Use delegating where appropriate to help you stay organized.

Jan Muller attended a seminar on how to get organized and felt very motivated to take control of several important areas of her office. She set out on her plan to identify what areas, if organized, would give her the most value. She worked to remove the clutter from those high payoff areas, and then she set up a schedule of several 15 to 20 minute sessions per week to follow the steps in her plan to organize those areas. After a month of committed effort, she had achieved her goal of setting up simple systems in the important areas of her office.

At this point Jan's story will go one of two ways:

Scenario A

Several weeks after completing her organizing tasks, Jan started to notice some deterioration in the quality of the systems she had set up. Things were starting to look disorganized again. She was juggling several projects at one time, and her time was at a premium. Therefore, she didn't give much thought to how well her "systems" were holding up until about two months later. One afternoon she objectively analyzed how she was maintaining the systems in her high payoff areas. She realized how almost everything looked the same as it did four months earlier before she attended the organizing seminar. "I did it again," she thought to herself. "I go to a seminar, get hooked on an idea, try it, and find out it was all a waste of time and energy . . . never again."

Scenario B

Jan realized quickly that if she wanted her systems to work for her, she would have to maintain them. She discovered and then cultivated several different maintenance habits that worked to keep her systems operating efficiently. Four months after attending the seminar her assessment was "Getting organized has been one of the most worthwhile ways I've spent my time."

- Jan noticed an improvement in her personal productivity; she seemed to be able to get more done in less time than she used to.

- Jan felt more self-confident in her work because she'd learned how to control her environment and was projecting a more professional image to her clients and co-workers. ■

MAINTAIN YOUR SYSTEMS

These story endings illustrate how it is possible to lose all or most of the benefits from getting organized if you overlook the importance of maintaining your systems. Maintenance is necessary to continue realizing the benefits from most things in your life:

- Once you work to build a strong personal relationship with someone, you know that to keep it strong you will have to maintain it regularly. List some of the maintenance activities necessary to keeping strong personal relationships: _____
_____
_____

- Your physical condition (diet, weight, exercise, etc.) requires a regular and consistent maintenance program. List some ways to maintain your physical condition: _____
_____
_____

- To keep your personal belongings (car, home, clothes, etc.) attractive and in good working order so you can get the full benefit from owning them, you must regularly and consistently maintain them. What are some of those maintenance activities? _____
_____
_____

Keeping operating efficiency in the areas that you have invested the time and energy to get organized also requires maintenance activities. The next section looks at some of these habits.

6

Practice Place Habits

This habit is based on the adage, "A place for everything, and everything in its place." If, for example, you consistently waste time everyday trying to find your keys, then you will save time by developing a place habit where you will put them in the same place when you walk into your home or office. If you truly develop a place habit of always putting the keys in a habitual place, you will rarely have to waste time looking for them. Time management experts cite a variety of statistics that support the premise that too few people practice place habits:

- Executives spend an average of 30 minutes a day (or a full workday per month) searching desktop piles for papers.
- The general population spends an average of one year of their lives searching for misplaced objects.

This may sound too obvious. However, many people set up a system— for example, a filing system—and then they never develop the habit of using that system as the place to put their papers. They continue with their old place habit of putting papers in random stacks on their desk instead of developing the new place habit of putting a piece of paper that is in their hands in the appropriate file (or in a folder for papers to be filed later). Then, the next time they need that piece of paper they do not have to rummage through the random piles on their desk; instead they can go directly to the appropriate file folder and find what they need quickly and efficiently.

Practice Time Habits

You will be more likely to complete routine tasks if you have set aside a scheduled time to do them. For example, if you need to read *The Wall Street Journal* daily, a time habit regarding the *WSJ* will help you avoid having piles of unread copies scattered around your office. Set aside a regular time each day when you will read what you need to read, clip articles or other information you need to save, and then discard the rest. Of course, time habits must be balanced with flexibility. Time habits, however, serve the purpose of keeping us on track most of the time. They are incorporated into our routine, whether at work or at home. If you practice a time habit for reading the *WSJ*, it will be the rule rather than the exception that you accomplish your reading requirements in a timely and consistent manner. Without time habits, many people are not consistent in carrying out the routine requirements of their work.

Establishing time habits is particularly helpful if you find yourself procrastinating on high payoff activities, such as maintaining one of your high payoff organizing systems. Establishing a time habit should help you overcome your procrastination. If, for example, your computer is an important tool in your work, you know you must perform regular maintenance tasks to keep your hard drive operating efficiently. Utilities programs, such as *PC Tools* and *Norton Utilities,* allow computer users to perform maintenance tasks such as data recovery and disk repair and speed and performance enhancement. Establishing a time habit, such as running the necessary utility programs on Monday mornings before beginning a new work week, would help computer users regularly perform this essential maintenance task.

Keep Your Organized Areas Uncluttered

You learned in Chapter 3, Unclutter Your Life, that you should unclutter an area **before** you work to get it organized. This guideline serves a dual purpose: it not only helps you **get** organized, but it also helps you **stay** organized. Make sure you regularly schedule unclutter time, a time habit, as a way to maintain your systems. The anticlutter principles that helped you before in setting up your system also will serve in keeping clutter from accumulating once your system is in use. The anticlutter principles are reviewed below with applications for maintaining a filing system:

- *Set limits.* Determine the maximum number of filing cabinets you will allow in your work area. Stay firm as long as possible. Remember that too often people who discover that they are out of filing space decide to order a new filing cabinet. A better approach would be to develop the habit of clearing out filing drawers every few months (or better yet to become more discriminating in what you save in the first place), in which case it would rarely be necessary to increase filing space. This principle applies to any storage space in your life: don't try to increase storage space until you've discarded or given away unused items that are filling up current space.

- *Analyze usage.* If you're like most people, 60 to 80 percent of the things you've filed in drawers are useless. In maintaining a filing system, it is critical not to save items that you will never use again. However, there is no way you can be 100 percent sure that you will use every item you put into your system; you will have to save some items because there's a chance you will need them. You may later find out that you don't need some of the items you've filed.

- *Be careful of oversentimentalizing.* There probably aren't too many things people save in a filing cabinet that are there for purely sentimental reasons. However, it is possible; so don't let sentimental items clutter your filing system.

- *Give items with value to someone who could still use them.* It is also rare to have items you discard from a filing system be of value to another person. Some of the papers, however, might be recyclable.

- *Handle things only once.* Put items that you determine must be saved in your filing system the first time you handle them. This may mean that you place the item in a folder "to be filed" as an intermediate step. It should never mean, however, that you place them on your desk and have them rotate from stack to stack for a month before they get where they're supposed to go. Because running back and forth between your desk and your filing system too often is an inefficient use of your time, the rule *handle things only once* needs to be revised when applied to your filing system. The revision reads *handle things only twice.* The extra step requires you to have an intermediate stopping place, such as a folder or stack of papers labeled Items to Be Filed, where during the week you place items that need to be filed, and then to set aside a time habit of when you (or an assistant) could file them into the permanent system. This method is obviously more efficient than running to your filing system every time you have a paper to be filed.

Use a Planner

Because most employees need a system to help them get the most use from their time, most people should invest money in a planner. Planners help you to integrate your calendar, important phone numbers, and "to do" shopping and reminder lists—all in one simple system. Lists can be helpful to track items to purchase when you stop by the store on the way home from work or to jot down a reminder to yourself to follow up on a promise made to a co-worker. Your calendar will help you organize your social activities, appointments, and birthdays and anniversaries you need to acknowledge. The simpler the system, the more likely it will be that you will be able to maintain it on a consistent basis without getting bogged down in a complicated, cumbersome system.

Use the 4-D Method for Handling Your Mail

Because mail can be a major source of clutter, as discussed in Chapter 3, it is critical that you not allow it to clutter your systems. Make a decision on what to do with each item the first time you look at it. The 4-D Method helps you make one of four choices for each item:

- **Don't open it.**
- **Discard it.**
- **Designate for action.**
- **Direct it.**

WHAT HABITS WILL HELP YOU STAY ORGANIZED?

6

In the following table listing, check the appropriate box indicating whether this is a habit you now practice regularly, rarely, or never. This self-assessment will help to identify your strong and weak areas and to focus your attention on maintenance habits you need to develop.

Maintenance Habit	Regularly	Rarely	Never
Practice place habits			
Practice time habits			
Keep your organized areas uncluttered			
Set limits			
Analyze usage			
Be careful of oversentimentalizing			
Give items with value to someone who could use them			
Handle things only once			
Use a planner			
Use the 4-D Method for handling your mail			

If you have checked "rarely" or "never" for any of these maintenance habits, consider which of those habits has the greatest potential to accommodate your work style and help you stay organized. Commit to try the one(s) you've selected by writing them on the line(s) below:

_____

_____

_____

DELEGATION: A SPECIAL TOOL

One reason some people find it difficult to stay organized is that they try to do more than is humanly possible. They try to do the work of two people and wonder why everything always seems to be in a state of chaos.

This can happen to mid-level executives or frontline employees who, because of organizational downsizing, are doing not only their own jobs but also the work of a colleague who was let go.

This can also happen to the working mother who tries to maintain a full-time job and meet the needs of her family with little or no assistance. She expects that she should be able to make sure her husband and children eat three well-balanced meals a day and always have a clean pair of socks to wear and that her home is always neat and orderly to receive unexpected visitors.

Delegating, or assigning a task in your area of responsibility to another person to complete, can be a special tool to help you stay organized. However, some people can't delegate. Not everyone identified in the preceding examples has access to a person to whom to delegate:

- Mid-level executives normally have extensive delegating authority.
- Frontline employees normally do not.
- Depending on her job, a working mother may or may not have delegating authority at work. Although delegating should be an option at home, it could be limited somewhat by the ages of her children or

the quality of the team relationship she and her husband have established. Another form of delegating available to working mothers is to hire various outside services to take care of some household responsibilities (for example, dry cleaners to wash and press shirts, a cleaning service to come in once a week to clean the house, and a tax service to complete the income taxes).

HOW TO DELEGATE

Some basic delegating principles include the following: **A delegator works to develop and empower subordinates (or children) by**

- Carefully evaluating tasks to be completed.
- Selecting who is best able to complete the task.
- Clearly communicating the essential information about the task.
  - The specifics of what is to be done.
  - The amount of authority you are delegating to the person to complete the task.
  - The deadline for completing the task.
- Set up appropriate control and feedback systems with a review date so you still hold on to the final responsibility to see that the task is carried out correctly and on time. With a new employee in whom you have not yet established a high enough level of confidence, for instance, you may want to set up a more regular control and feedback system than you would with a long-time employee in whom you have a great deal of confidence.

To help determine what to delegate, list your activities according to the following categories:

- Tasks you must do and should never delegate (a supervisory example is that you should handle delicate disciplinary problems and not delegate the task because it is one you'd rather not deal with).
- Tasks that you should do but that someone could assist you in doing.

- Tasks that you could do but that someone else could do if given the opportunity.

Consider these pointers on how to use delegating effectively:

- Instead of falling into the trap of saying, "If you want a job done right, you have to do it yourself," develop your delegating skills so that you will be able to say instead, "If you want a job done right, you will delegate it to the person best able to handle it."
- Have enough confidence in your subordinates to trust them with a task that is normally your responsibility. Be prepared to take some risks and be prepared that no one will do the task exactly the same way as you would.
- Avoid delegating *only* unpleasant tasks.
- Allow employees additional time to complete delegated responsibilities.
- The time needed to train somebody pays big dividends in the future by freeing up your time to pursue other responsibilities.
- A delegated task changes from being totally your responsibility to becoming a shared responsibility: the subordinate becomes responsible to you, while you retain responsibility to higher management.

The Connection to Staying Organized.   Here are some examples of organizing tasks that could be delegated:

- Keeping your filing up-to-date.
- Clerical tasks related to projects you're working on, for example, typing a list of names, addresses, and telephone numbers for all people related to the project, or making phone calls to find price and product information from several vendors and presenting the information in an organized format that will help you make decisions more quickly.
- On the home front: even young children are great at folding laundry, loading the dishwasher, helping to rake leaves, and making their

own beds. Get them started young so they get used to helping with household chores.

Identify Organizing Tasks to Delegate

For each item you list, complete the chart information (the best person for the task, how much training will be involved, when does the task need to be done—this can be a deadline date or it can be the frequency with which the task has to be done, such as weekly or monthly—and explanation of any control and feedback systems).

Task	Person	Training	Deadline/ Frequency	Control/ Feedback

6

Chapter Checkpoints

✓ Maintenance is necessary to keep systems working efficiently.

✓ Five maintenance habits help you stay organized and realize the benefits of your systems:
- Practice place habits.
- Practice time habits.
- Keep your organized areas uncluttered.
- Use a planner.
- Use the 4-D Method for handling your mail.

✓ Delegate when appropriate to help maintain your systems.

7 | Be Only as Organized as You Need to Be

This chapter will help you to:

- Understand the meaning of *level of organization*.
- Categorize your high payoff areas as space, information, or time resources.
- Relate the kind of work you do with the way you work.
- Develop a plan of action to attain your best level of organization.
- Regularly assess your level of organization to make sure it's still meeting your needs.

David Grant tends to feel intimidated when he is around Jeff Sharkey. It's hard for him not to seem lacking when he compares his level of organization with Jeff's. Jeff projects an image of total control. His office appears in perfect order 99.9 percent of the time. His recollection is flawless when anybody asks him for anything; he practically has the item in hand before the person has finished describing what he or she needs. In contrast, David's office has a much more lived-in look and would never be featured in *Office Beautiful* magazine. Jeff's day-timer is neat and orderly and is his indispensable aid in keeping appointments, phone numbers, to-do lists, and other information at his fingertips. David, on the other hand, tried using a day-timer, but gave up on it after repeatedly misplacing it.

Even though David has been making improvements in being organized, he gets discouraged when he compares himself with the model of perfection that he has to work with every day. It seems that the more David tries to be organized like Jeff the more discouraged he gets. ∎

David's situation illustrates the final guideline of *Getting and Staying Organized*. David's mistake is a common one. Rather than being as organized as he needs to be, he's trying to be as organized as someone else needs to be. David, in fact, is in the best position to know what level of organization is best for him. Sure, it's a good idea for him to observe the ways others are organized. That's a good way to pick up many good pointers. He got into trouble, however, when he let another person's level of organization dictate the level of organization for him. As you will see in the next section, level of organization is an individual matter. Chances are that even if David were somehow magically able to create a work environment that was exactly like Jeff's, David probably would not be comfortable or satisfied working at Jeff's level of organization. Everyone must determine his or her own level of organization.

DEFINING LEVEL OF ORGANIZATION

You learned in grasping Chapter 2 that if you identify the high payoff areas to organize, the 20 percent you use most often, you will realize 80 percent of the benefits you can derive from getting organized. Identifying high payoff areas tells you only *what* to get organized. It focuses your attention on the areas requiring organization so you can use the resources contained in those areas efficiently (so they're not wasted) and effectively (to help you accomplish tasks). In contrast, the *degree or level of organization* you will need in those high payoff areas is a matter of your own work style.

Several factors will come into play to help you determine your most comfortable and appropriate level of organization.

What Kind of Work Do You Do?

▪ *Dealing face to face with the public.* If you regularly have clients, suppliers, or other people outside your organization visit your office, you need a higher level of organization than a person whose office rarely has outside visitors. You would expect, for example, that the public relations staff would place a higher priority on the appearance and organization level of their offices than would the director of maintenance. The PR staff would regularly receive visitors, while the maintenance staff would rarely have visitors.

- *Having support staff.* If others in your office will access the filing system in your office, your system must be at a higher level of organization than the filing system belonging to a person who has no one else using it.

How Do You Work?

- *Characteristics of the work environment that affect your productivity.* Some people find it nearly impossible to get things done when their surroundings become too disorderly. They become frustrated and must stop what they're doing long enough to restore order to their surroundings. Others find a bit of disorderliness necessary for their creative juices to flow, and they feel stifled or inhibited when they feel obligated to keep things too precisely neat and orderly while they're working.

- *Personal preferences.* Some people derive great satisfaction from having the most colorful filing system in town; they would never dream of using drab manila folders. They're the ones who not only buy the five-pound planners with 15 sections in them but also actually use them. Others just are not into color coding and alphabetizing everything they own. They do not require that their systems impress anybody else; utility is all they require.

YOUR BEST LEVEL OF ORGANIZATION

When you examine the high payoff areas you've determined are your 20 percent to get organized (see your list on page 49), you will see that they fall into three categories of resources:

Space: These can be specific storage areas (such as closets and drawers) or things that represent your working environment and your effort to make that environment both functional and pleasing to the eye (such as your desktop area).

Information: Other areas relate to systems you have established to keep your information up to date and easily accessible (such as a rotary card file). This category also refers to systems you have established for productive paperwork and work flow procedures.

Time: Some systems, such as to-do lists, scheduling, goal setting, and project management, help you use your time more wisely.

■ Just Do It!

Using the chart that follows, identify those high payoff areas you listed on page 49 relating to each of the three resource categories described above. Based on the kind of work you do and the way you work, determine what level of organization is the most appropriate for each.

7

Resource Category	Your High Payoff Areas	Level of Organization Standard		
		Low	Medium	High
Space				
Information				
Time				

■ Attaining Your Level of Organization

Refer to the chart you have just completed and put a check mark next to each high payoff area for which you use a system to meet the level of organization standard you set. Next, circle those areas on your chart for which you have not yet established a system or need to establish a better one to allow you to have the level of organization standard for that area.

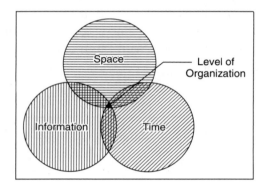

DEVELOP A PLAN OF ACTION

The next step is to develop a plan of action to reach the level of organization standard you have established for each of your high payoff areas. Select one circled area from your chart for which you want to develop a plan of action and complete the chart on the pages that follow.

ACTION PLAN

1. I am committed to getting the following _____ (fill in
   space, information, or *time*) resource organized at a _____
   (fill in *low, medium,* or *high*) level of organization standard.

2. I will complete this goal by _____ (fill in specific date).

3. I anticipate that there may be some obstacles that will stand in the
   way of my accomplishing this goal. If I list those obstacles (e.g., procrastination or clutter) along with how I anticipate dealing with them
   (e.g., just do it; break task into manageable parts), I will be better
   prepared to deal with them effectively if they interfere with reaching
   my goal.

Potential Obstacle	Counter Strategy

4. If there are any people who can help me organize this area, I will
   list their names here (e.g., assistant, co-worker) and designate specifics about how I will get them involved. _____

   _____

5. If organizing this area requires purchasing any organizing aids
   (such as a planner or file folders), I will list those aids here:

   _____

   _____

6. What are the specific steps I will follow to complete this organizing project? When will I set aside or schedule the necessary time—appointments with myself—to work to achieve my goal? What will I accomplish during each scheduled appointment? How many appointments do I project will be needed to complete my goal? (Review pages 49–51 for an example of how to clarify the steps you will follow.) _____

_____

_____

_____

_____

_____

7. When I complete this organizing project, these are the benefits I expect to realize. (Review the introductory chapter to remind yourself of some of the benefits listed there, such as experiencing improved personal productivity, being able to get more done in less time, improving your self-confidence as you learn to control your environment instead of your environment controlling you, and projecting an improved professional image to clients and co-workers.)

_____

_____

_____

_____

7

ASSESSING YOUR OVERALL LEVEL OF ORGANIZATION

You are, no doubt, interested in realizing long-term benefits from the time you have invested in reading and studying this book, not to mention the time you have spent or you will spend in getting your high payoff areas organized. Chapter 6, Stay Organized, presented several maintenance habits repeated below that can keep you from falling back into your former disorganized ways.

- Practice place habits.
- Practice time habits.
- Keep your organized areas uncluttered.
- Use a planner.
- Use the 4-D Method for handling your mail.
- Delegate when appropriate.

7

Another dimension to realizing long-term benefits is that few people's jobs are the same today as they were even six months ago. Some examples of the ways jobs change follow:

- You're no longer doing some of the things you used to do.
- You're asked to do more than you used to do.
- You've been given new responsibilities.
- The equipment you use to do your job has been updated.
- You've moved to a new location.
- You have a new boss who has a new way of doing things.
- You're using computer software you didn't use six months ago.
- You've been promoted or relocated to a totally different job or maybe even gone to a different company.

Take a few moments to think about the changes that have taken place in your job over the past 6 to 12 months and list them below:

_____

_____

_____

_____

_____

_____

As the conditions of your work change, you will need to reevaluate your level of organization to make sure you're keeping pace with the changes in your job. Here are some questions to consider:

- Do I need to drop from my list high payoff areas that are no longer high payoff in light of the changes in my work?
- What new high payoff areas do I need to add to my list?
- Do any levels of organization standards need to be adjusted? For example, in your old job you might have had very few outside visitors in your office and therefore used a low level of organization for your office. In your new position, you have more contact with the public and need to raise your level of organization standard to reflect that change.
- Do I have adequate time, space, and information systems in place to handle the changes in any of these resources?

Answering these periodically, or when you have any significant changes in your job, will ensure that you're getting the most out of your organizing efforts.

7

Chapter Checkpoints

✓ Be only as organized as you, not others, need to be.

✓ Your level of organization (low, medium, or high) is determined by the kind of work you do and the way you work.

✓ The systems you have in place are designed to help you organize your space, information, or time resources.

✓ When you develop a plan of action to achieve your level of organization goals, you will need to
  - Commit yourself to a specific goal to be completed by a specific date.
  - Anticipate obstacles that might interfere with achieving your goal and develop counter-strategies that will help you deal with each obstacle.
  - Identify the people who might be able to help you achieve your goal.
  - Consider whether you will need to purchase any organizing aids.
  - Develop a plan that defines when you will complete the steps necessary to reach your goal.
  - Spell out what's in it for you when you complete this organizing project.

✓ Make adjustments to your level of organization to keep pace with changes in your job.

Post-Test

1. Efficiency is _____, while effectiveness is _____.
   a. Getting the job done in a timely fashion; doing the job with no mistakes.
   b. Doing the job with no mistakes; getting the job done in a timely fashion.
   c. Using your resources to their maximum capacity; accomplishing a task or reaching a goal.
   d. Accomplishing a task or reaching a goal; using your resources to their maximum capacity.

2. What can organizing skills do for you?
   a. Improve your personal productivity.
   b. Improve your self-confidence.
   c. Help you to project a more professional image to clients and co-workers.
   d. All of the above.

3. Which statement is *not* true about the 80–20 Rule?
   a. 80% of the value comes from 20% of the resources.
   b. The 20% you get organized that results in 80% of the value must qualify as low payoff areas for the 80–20 Rule to work.
   c. Another name for the 80–20 Rule is the Pareto Principle.
   d. The relationship may not always be exactly 80–20; it may be 70–30 or 85–15.

4. Which *two* answers below represent the two tendencies that cause us to accumulate clutter:
   a. Hanging on to unnecessary things.
   b. Putting off making decisions.
   c. Filling up available storage space.
   d. Buying on impulse.

5. Which Anticlutter Principle relates to developing a habit to make a decision right away where an item should go or who should get it?

   a. Set limits.

   b. Analyze usage.

   c. Be careful of oversentimentalizing.

   d. Handle things only once.

6. When you are procrastinating because the task is too difficult, which counter strategy can help you overcome your procrastination?

   a. Just do it!

   b. Call a friend to talk you out of procrastinating.

   c. Break the task into several smaller tasks that are more easily achieved.

   d. Stop eating until after you've completed the difficult task.

7. Based on the guideline Establish a Simple System, circle two answers below that represent the two requirements for your organizing effort to qualify as simple.

   a. You use color-coding.

   b. Others who may need to use it will understand it.

   c. You base it on an alphabetical arrangement.

   d. You won't have to spend a lot of time maintaining it.

8. Which principle presented under Establish a Simple System applies to using a "to do" list to consolidate your telephone messages, reminders, and other tasks to accomplish?

   a. It is easy for you to maintain.

   b. The most-used items are in the easiest-to-get-at locations.

   c. Materials and equipment used to complete common tasks are grouped together.

   d. You learn from co-workers about the systems that have worked for them.

9. Bryan decides that Tuesday and Thursday mornings from 9 to 10:30 are the best times for him to commit to answering correspondence. Which maintenance habit is Bryan using to help him maintain his system to keep up-to-date on correspondence?

    a. Practice place habits.

    b. Practice time habits.

    c. Keep your organized areas uncluttered.

    d. Use a planner.

10. Which is *not* a factor in determining your most comfortable and appropriate level of organization?

    a. What works well for the most organized person you know.

    b. Whether you deal face to face with the public.

    c. Whether you have support staff.

    d. Your personal preferences.

Business Skills Express Series

This growing series of books addresses a broad range of key business skills and topics to meet the needs of employees, human resource departments, and training consultants.

To obtain information about these and other Business Skills Express books, please call Irwin Professional Publishing toll free at 1-800-634-3966.

Effective Performance Management
ISBN   1-55623-867-3

Hiring the Best
ISBN   1-55623-865-7

Writing that Works
ISBN   1-55623-856-8

Customer Service Excellence
ISBN   1-55623-969-6

Writing for Business Results
ISBN   1-55623-854-1

Powerful Presentation Skills
ISBN   1-55623-870-3

Meetings that Work
ISBN   1-55623-866-5

Effective Teamwork
ISBN   1-55623-880-0

Time Management
ISBN   1-55623-888-6

Assertiveness Skills
ISBN   1-55623-857-6

Motivation at Work
ISBN   1-55623-868-1

Overcoming Anxiety at Work
ISBN   1-55623-869-X

Positive Politics at Work
ISBN   1-55623-879-7

Telephone Skills at Work
ISBN   1-55623-858-4

Managing Conflict at Work
ISBN   1-55623-890-8

The New Supervisor: Skills for Success
ISBN   1-55623-762-6

The *Americans with Disabilities Act*: What Supervisors Need to Know
ISBN   1-55623-889-4

Managing the Demands of Work and Home
ISBN   0-7863-0221-6

Effective Listening Skills
ISBN   0-7863-0102-4

Goal Management at Work
ISBN   0-7863-0225-9

Positive Attitudes at Work
ISBN   0-7863-0100-8

Supervising the Difficult Employee
ISBN   0-7863-0219-4

Cultural Diversity in the Workplace
ISBN   0-7863-0125-2

Managing Change in the Workplace
ISBN   0-7863-0162-7

Negotiating for Business Results
ISBN   0-7863-0114-7

Practical Business Communication
ISBN   0-7863-0227-5

High Performance Speaking
ISBN   0-7863-0222-4

Delegation Skills
ISBN   0-7863-0105-9

Coaching Skills: A Guide for Supervisors
ISBN   0-7863-0220-8

Customer Service and the Telephone
ISBN   0-7863-0224-0

Creativity at Work
ISBN   0-7863-0223-2

Effective Interpersonal Relationships
ISBN   0-7863-0255-0

The Participative Leader
ISBN   0-7863-0252-6

Building Customer Loyalty
ISBN   0-7863-0253-4

Getting and Staying Organized
ISBN   0-7863-0254-2

Moving Meetings
ISBN   0-7863-0333-6

Total Quality Selling
ISBN   0-7863-0324-7

Business Etiquette
ISBN   0-7863-0323-9

Empowering Employees
ISBN   0-7863-314-X

Training Skills for Supervisors
ISBN   0-7863-0313-1

Multicultural Customer Service
ISBN   0-7863-0332-8